954.03   85/3418

920   BIOGRAPHY
GAN

W9-CNL-468

GANDHI, MAHATMA
"   Mohandas

**This book is to be returned on or before
the last date stamped below.**

LIBREX

MOHANDAS
GANDHI

Catherine Bush

Burke Publishing Company Limited
LONDON ∗ TORONTO ∗ NEW YORK

First published in the United States of America 1985
© 1985 by Chelsea House Publishers,
a division of Chelsea House Educational Communications, Inc.
Introduction copyright © 1985 by Arthur M. Schlesinger, jr.

This edition first published 1988
New material in this edition
© Burke Publishing Company Limited 1988

ACKNOWLEDGEMENTS
The Author and Publishers are grateful to the following organizations for
permission to reproduce copyright illustrations in this book:
    AP/Wide World Photos, BBC Hulton Picture Library. UPI and Bettmann
    Archive.

CIP data
Bush, Catherine
    Mohandas Gandhi. — (World leaders: past and present)
    1. Gandhi, M. K.
    2. Statesmen—India—Biography
    I. Title   II. Series
    954.03'5'0924   DS481.G3

ISBN 0 222 01204 8 Hardbound
ISBN 0 222 01223 4 Paperback

Burke Publishing Company Limited
Pegasus House, 116-120 Golden Lane, London EC1Y 0TL, England
Printed in England by Purnell Book Production Limited.

CONTENTS

WORLD LEADERS   PAST AND PRESENT

Konrad Adenauer
Alexander the Great
Mark Antony
King Arthur
Kemal Atatürk
Clement Attlee
Menachem Begin
David Ben Gurion
Bismarck
Léon Blum
Símon Bolívar
Cesare Borgia
Willy Brandt
Leonid Brezhnev
Julius Ceasar
Calvin
Fidel Castro
Catherine the Great
Charlemagne
Chiang Kai-Shek
Chou En-Lai
Winston Churchill
Clemenceau
Cleopatra
Cortes
Cromwell
Danton
Charles De Gaulle
De Valera
Disraeli
Dwight D. Eisenhower
Eleanor of Aquitaine
Queen Elizabeth I

Ferdinand and Isabella
Franco
Frederick the Great
Indira Gandhi
Mohandas K. Gandhi
Garibaldi
Genghis Khan
Gladstone
Dag Hammarskjöld
Henry VIII
Henry of Navarre
Hindenburg
Adolf Hitler
Ho Chi Minh
King Hussein
Ivan the Terrible
Andrew Jackson
Thomas Jefferson
Joan of Arc
Pope John XXIII
Lyndon Johnson
Benito Juárez
John F. Kennedy
Jomo Kenyatta
Ayatollah Khomeini
Nikita Khrushchev
Martin Luther King
Henry Kissinger
Vladimir Lenin
Abraham Lincoln
Lloyd George
Louis XIV
Martin Luther
Judas Maccabeus

Mao Tse Tung
Mary, Queen of Scots
Golda Meir
Metternich
Benito Mussolini
Napoleon
Jamal Nasser
Jawalharlal Nehru
Nero
Nicholas II
Richard Nixon
Kwame Nkrumah
Pericles
Juan Perón
Muammar Qaddafi
Robespierre
Eleanor Roosevelt
Franklin D. Roosevelt
Theodore Roosevelt
Anwar Sadat
Sun Yat-Sen
Joseph Stalin
Tamerlane
Margaret Thatcher
Iosif Tito
Leon Trotsky
Pierre Trudeau
Harry S. Truman
Queen Victoria
George Washington
Chaim Weizmann
Woodrow Wilson
Xerxes

Further titles in preparation

ON LEADERSHIP
Arthur M. Schlesinger, jr.

LEADERSHIP, it may be said, is really what makes the world go round. Love no doubt smooths the passage; but love is a private transaction between consenting adults. Leadership is a public transaction with history. The idea of leadership affirms the capacity of individuals to move, inspire and mobilize masses of people so that they act together in pursuit of an end. Sometimes leadership serves good purposes, sometimes bad; but whether the end is benign or evil, great leaders are those men and women who leave their personal stamp on history.

Now, the very concept of leadership implies the proposition that individuals can make a difference. This proposition has never been universally accepted. From classical times to the present day, eminent thinkers have regarded individuals as no more than the agents and pawns of larger forces, whether the gods and goddesses of the ancient world or, in the modern era, race, class, nation, the dialectic, the will of the people, the spirit of the times, history itself. Against such forces, the individual dwindles into insignificance.

So contends the thesis of historical determinism. Tolstoy's great novel *War and Peace* offers a famous statement of the case. Why, Tolstoy asked, did millions of men in the Napoleonic wars, denying their human feelings and their common sense, move back and forth across Europe slaughtering their fellows? "The war," Tolstoy answered, "was bound to happen simply because it was bound to happen." All prior history predetermined it. As for leaders, they, Tolstoy said, "are but the labels that serve to give a name to an end and, like labels, they have the least possible connection with the event." The greater the leader, "the more conspicuous the inevitability and the predestination of every act he commits." The leader, said Tolstoy, is "the slave of history".

Determinism takes many forms. Marxism is the determinism of class, Nazism the determinism of race. But the idea of men and women as the slaves of history runs athwart the deepest human instincts. Rigid determinism abolishes the idea of human freedom—the assumption of free choice that underlies every move we make, every word we speak, every thought we think. It abolishes the idea of human responsibility, since it is manifestly unfair to reward or punish people for actions that are by definition beyond their control. No one can live consistently by any deterministic creed. The Marxist states prove this themselves by their extreme susceptibility to the cult of leadership.

More than that, history refutes the idea that individuals make no difference. In December 1931 a British politician crossing Park Avenue in New York City between 76th and 77th Streets around ten-thirty at night looked in the wrong direction and was knocked down by a speeding car—a moment, he later recalled, of a man aghast, a world aglare: "I do not understand why I was not broken like an eggshell or squashed like a gooseberry." Fourteen months later an American politician, sitting in an open car in Miami, Florida, was fired on by an assassin; the man beside him was hit. Those who believe that individuals make no difference to history might well ponder whether the next two decades would have been the same, had Mario Contasini's car killed Winston Churchill in 1931 and had Giuseppe Zangara's bullet killed Franklin Roosevelt in 1933. Suppose, in addition, that Adolf Hitler had been killed in the street fighting during the Munich *Putsch* of 1923 and that Lenin had died of typhus during the First World War. What would the 20th century be like now?

For better or for worse, individuals do make a difference. "The notion that a people can run itself and its affairs anonymously," wrote the philosopher William James, "is now well known to be the silliest of absurdities. Mankind does nothing save through initiatives on the part of inventors, great or small, and imitation by the rest of us—these are the sole factors in human progress. Individuals of genius show the way, and set the patterns, which common people then adopt and follow."

Leadership, James suggests, means leadership in thought as well as in action. In the long run, leaders in thought may well make the greater difference to the world. But, as Woodrow Wilson once said, "Those only are leaders of men, in the general eye, who lead in action . . . It is at their hands that new thought gets its translation into the crude language of deeds." Leaders in thought often invent in solitude and obscurity, leaving to later generations the tasks of imitation. Leaders in action—the leaders portrayed in this series—have to be effective in their own time.

And they cannot be effective by themselves. They must act in response to the rhythms of their age. Their genius must be adapted, in a phrase of William James's, "to the receptivities of the moment". Leaders are useless without followers. "There goes the mob," said the French politician hearing a clamour in the streets. "I am their leader. I must follow them." Great leaders turn the inchoate emotions of the mob to purposes of their own. They seize on the opportunities of their time, the hopes, fears, frustrations, crises, potentialities. They succeed when events have prepared the way for them, when the community is waiting to be aroused, when they can provide the clarifying and organizing ideas. Leadership ignites the circuit between the individual and the mass and thereby alters history. It may alter history for better or for worse. Leaders have been responsible for the most extravagant follies and most monstrous crimes that have beset suffering humanity. They have also been vital in such gains as humanity has made in individual freedom, religious and racial tolerance, social justice and respect for human rights.

There is no sure way to tell in advance who is going to lead for good and who for evil. But a glance at the gallery of men and women in *World Leaders—Past and Present* suggests some useful tests.

One test is this: do leaders lead by force or by persuasion? By command or by consent? Through most of history leadership was exercised by the divine right of authority. The duty of followers was to defer and to obey. *"Their's not to reason why,/Their's but to do and die."* On occasion, as with the so-called "enlightened despots" of the 18th century in Europe, absolutist leadership was animated by humane purposes. More often, absolutism nourished the passion for domination, land, gold and conquest and resulted in tyranny.

The great revolution of modern times has been the revolution of equality. The idea that all people should be equal in their legal condition has undermined the old structures of authority, hierarchy and deference. The revolution of equality has had two contrary effects on the nature of leadership. For equality, as Alexis de Tocqueville pointed out in his great study *Democracy in America,* might mean equality in servitude as well as equality in freedom.

"I know of only two methods of establishing equality in the political world," Tocqueville wrote. "Rights must be given to every citizen, or none at all to anyone . . . save one, who is the master of all." There was no middle ground "between the sovereignty of all and the absolute power of one man". In his astonishing prediction of 20th-century totalitarian dictatorship, Tocqueville explained how the revolution of equality could lead to the *Führerprinzip* and more terrible absolutism than the world had ever known.

But when rights are given to every citizen and the sovereignty of all is established, the problem of leadership takes a new form, becomes more exacting than ever before. It is easy to issue commands and enforce them by the rope and the stake, the concentration camp and the *gulag.* It is much harder to use argument and achievement to overcome opposition and win consent. The Founding Fathers of the United States understood the difficulty. They believed that history had given them the opportunity to decide, as Alexander Hamilton wrote in the first Federalist Paper, whether men are indeed capable of basing government on "reflection and choice, or whether they are forever destined to depend . . . on accident and force."

Government by reflection and choice called for a new style of leadership and a new quality of followership. It required leaders to be responsive to popular concerns, and it required followers to be active and informed participants in the process. Democracy does not eliminate emotion from politics; sometimes it fosters demagogy; but it is confident that, as the greatest of democratic leaders put it, you cannot fool all of the people all of the time. It measures leadership by results and retires those who overreach or falter or fail.

It is true that in the long run despots are measured by results too. But they can postpone the day of judgement, sometimes indefinitely, and in the meantime they can do infinite harm. It is also true that democracy is no guarantee of virtue and intelligence in government, for the voice of the people is not necessarily the voice of God. But democracy, by assuring the rights of opposition, offers built-in resistance to the evils inherent in absolutism. As the theologian Reinhold Niebuhr summed it up, "Man's capacity for justice makes democracy possible, but man's inclination to injustice makes democracy necessary."

A second test for leadership is the end for which power is sought. When leaders have as their goal the supremacy of a master race or the promotion of totalitarian revolution or the acquisition and exploitation of colonies or the protection of greed and privilege or the preservation of personal power, it is likely that their leadership will do little to advance the cause of humanity. When their goal is the abolition of slavery, the liberation of women, the enlargement of opportunity for the poor and powerless, the extension of equal rights to racial minorities, the defence of the freedoms of expression and opposition, it is likely that their leadership will increase the sum of human liberty and welfare.

Leaders have done great harm to the world. They have also conferred great benefits. You will find both sorts in this series. Even "good" leaders must be regarded with a certain wariness. Leaders are not demigods; they put on their trousers one leg after another just like ordinary mortals. No leader is infallible, and every leader needs to be reminded of this at regular intervals. Irreverence irritates leaders but is their salvation. Unquestioning submission corrupts leaders and demeans followers. Making a cult of a leader is always a mistake. Fortunately hero worship generates its own antidote. "Every hero," said Emerson, "becomes a bore at last."

The signal benefit the great leaders confer is to embolden the rest of us to live according to our own best selves, to be active, insistent, and resolute in affirming our own sense of things. For great leaders attest to the reality of human freedom against the supposed inevitabilities of history. And they attest to the wisdom and power that may lie within the most unlikely of us, which is why Abraham Lincoln remains the supreme example of great leadership. A great leader, said Emerson, exhibits new possibilities to all humanity. "We feed on genius . . . Great men exist that there may be greater men."

Great leaders, in short, justify themselves by emancipating and empowering their followers. So humanity struggles to master its destiny, remembering with Alexis de Tocqueville: "It is true that around every man a fatal circle is traced beyond which he cannot pass; but within the wide verge of that circle he is powerful and free; as it is with man, so with communities."

ARTHUR M. SCHLESINGER JR.
New York

1

Gandhi's India

It was a strange way to launch a national rebellion. On April 6, a small and frail old man, wearing only a peasant's homespun loincloth, walked to the Indian coast, stooped down, and picked up a few grains of sea salt. He was not the leader of a political party. Nor did he hold any position of power. He wore little round glasses, carried a staff and a pocket watch on a chain; these were almost all of his worldly possessions. Yet during the 24 days that he and his band of followers spent marching to the coast, thousands of fellow Indians came to swell their ranks. Peasants threw flowers in their path and sprinkled water on the ground to stop the dust from rising. And when the old man picked up the salt between his fingers, word travelled like lightning through India and echoed around the world.

India had waited two months for this signal from Mohandas Gandhi to renew the struggle for independence. When India's political leaders first heard that Gandhi intended to break the law which gave the British government in India a monopoly over the salt trade, they were baffled. They had asked him to lead them to independence. Why give attention to such a minor issue at this crucial time? The viceroy, the British head of state in India, must have shared their opinion. He did not even bother to stop Gandhi.

I am not a saint who has strayed into politics. I am a politician who is trying to become a saint.
—GANDHI

A sample of the homespun cotton cloth which Gandhi urged his followers to make and wear. The printed image of a spinning wheel was a Gandhi trademark, signifying native Indian manufacture using traditional equipment, not industrial factory methods.

Gandhi works at his spinning wheel in 1930. Gandhi's adoption of the craft of spinning symbolized his commitment to the political and economic regeneration of India on purely Indian terms and the rejection of British concepts and influence.

India has given birth to many religions, and temples abound throughout the country. This temple in Calcutta, now used by Buddhists, was originally built by members of the Jain religion, who believed that a perfect human soul could itself create and morally regulate the universe.

Both sides underestimated this remarkable man. Gandhi had his finger on the pulse of his country and its people. Salt was essential to the diet of India's poor labourers, who comprised the majority of the Indian people. They needed it to replenish the body's supplies lost in perspiration as they worked in the sweltering heat.

Even if the politicians were baffled, the people could immediately see that the freedom to produce salt should be their right. Gandhi believed that a country's power stemmed from the will of its people, not from its political leaders, and that India could win its independence from the British only after the people stopped fearing their oppressive rulers. Disobeying the salt laws freed the Indian people from fear.

If Gandhi had just made a speech, instead of marching to the coast to pick up salt in his own hands, he would never have had the impact he did.

Gandhi recognized that an act can have greater power than words.

Gandhi was an astute statesman. He was at the same time a living example of his belief in truth, tolerance, and nonviolence. These principles governed all his actions. For him, personal and political action could not be separated any more than religious and political philosophies could.

The people of India worshipped Gandhi as a holy man, calling him *Mahatma*, which means "great soul". They followed him in his struggle to win independence by nonviolent means. They went to jail and let themselves be beaten because they believed in him, even if they did not always understand or agree with his ideas. Politician and saint,

The clock tower of Khoja Jamat Khana, a Muslim religious and social centre, soars above this street in Bombay. Gandhi worked throughout his life to bring Hindus and Muslims together, yet violent conflict between the two religions still continues.

Bombay's Victoria rail station is one of India's most spectacular colonial buildings. British engineers planned and supervised the construction of India's vast railway system, much of which is still in use.

Gandhi was a man full of contradictions, and the reaction that he inspired was extraordinary—in India and beyond. Around the world people have responded to his example and adopted his method of political protest without violence.

The task of winning independence for India required more than just driving out the British, as Gandhi saw. Ironically, it was the British presence that had largely succeeded in uniting the vast Indian subcontinent, which was divided internally by region, language, religion, and social status. Linking the people in a common cause, even independence, was no easy matter.

India is nearly as large as all of Europe and 15 times the size of Britain, although until the end of World War II that tiny island ruled an empire that stretched around the globe. Then, as now, most of India's population lived in its 700,000 villages and worked the soil by hand. Droughts and monsoons continually threatened the peasants' livelihood. Famine and disease claimed many lives, sometimes millions in a year. People suffered not only from poverty but lack of sanitation. Villages had open sewage and no running water. Most people did not live to be more than 30 years old. And yet India was troubled with an enormous population and rapid rate of population growth—problems which continue today. In Gandhi's lifetime the population leaped from 200 to 400 million.

India is a country characterized by such extremes. At the other end of the scale from the thousands of villages were huge cities like Calcutta and Bombay. The teeming, filthy slums trapped people in even worse conditions than in the country. But the extreme poverty of country and city was matched by incredible wealth, which reached its heights in the courts of the maharajahs, India's native princes.

Religious differences also divided India's population and were the source of vicious conflict, especially between the two largest religious groups, the Hindus, who formed 70% of the population, and the Muslims, 25%.

The ruins of the Chutter Munzil, a former royal palace which was blown up by the rebel forces during the Indian Mutiny in 1857, when native Indian army soldiers mutinied against their British officers and the British colonial government. The British took savage reprisals against the rebels, showing no mercy.

Calcutta's Memorial Arch was built in honour of England's King Edward VII. The inscription (written in Latin) reads "Edward VII King and Emperor".

Hinduism was brought to India over 3,000 years ago. As a religion, Hinduism is flexible and incorporates many different forms of worship, unlike strictly organized religions such as Christianity, Judaism, or Islam. On the other hand, all Hindus are bound by a rigid class system which divides Hindu society into four major classes or castes. These were originally related to occupation, and in the past marriage and even dining were prohibited between members of different castes. The *Brah-*

mans, or priestly caste, ranked highest; below them were the *Kshatriyas*, formerly princes and soldiers; next came the *Vaisyas*, farmers, merchants and officials; the lowest caste was composed of the *Sudras*, or labourers.

Below even the *Sudras* were the untouchables, so called because no caste Hindu could touch them or anything that had come in contact with them— even their shadows—without pollution. They were forced to live in the worst parts of terrible slums or on the outskirts of villages where they had to drink and wash in already dirty water. They did the most menial and degrading work, like cleaning up refuse or removing dead bodies. Gandhi called untouchability a blot on Hinduism that had to be wiped out.

Yet the belief in reincarnation shared by all Hindus had long supported the caste system and

A statue of Gandhi shown comforting an untouchable child. Gandhi was deeply concerned with the plight of the untouchable caste throughout his life.

A monument marking the spot where 123 British men, women, and children died of thirst, starvation, and disease when Indian rebels kept them in close confinement in 1756. Their terrible ordeal has become known as "The Black Hole of Calcutta".

made it very hard to overturn. The form a person takes in this life is determined by the way he or she behaved in the life before. If you were born an untouchable, you were atoning for sins committed in your last life. If you accepted your postion, you would rise to a higher level of existence in your next life. You went on being reborn until you reached spiritual purity. This belief gave even untouchables a reason not to fight for change.

In the ninth century, invading Muslims from the Moghul empire brought the Islamic religion to Hindu India and took over political control. In the 16th century, Europeans began to penetrate the country on commercial expeditions. First came the Portuguese, then the Dutch, the French, and the English. By the 18th century, the British East India

Company held a monopoly on trade, exporting India's spices, textiles, and raw materials. Soon the British began to assume political and military supremacy. By the mid-19th century, the British government had taken over political control. It governed the rule of pro-British native princes.

The British helped unite India with roads and railway lines. English became the common language among Indians of different regions. To get ahead Indians had to try to be as "British" as possible.

Initially, the British had wanted to buy Indian goods. But by the 19th century, with the rise of industrialized manufacture in England, the British made India a market for British goods, discouraging Indian industry and sapping the country of capital. Gandhi was born into an India still troubled by age-old social and religious divisions, weakened by economic exploitation, and trapped under the thumb of colonial rule. A mere few thousand British civil servants ruled over 300 million Indians, India searched for the strength to break free.

Calcutta's famous "Gateway to India", one of the greatest imperial monuments ever constructed by the British, is dedicated to the memory of Britain's King George V (d.1936).

2

Beginnings

Although he wore only a loincloth and identified himself with the poor, Mohandas Gandhi was born in 1869 in a comfortable three-storey house shared by his father, his father's brothers, and their families. He was the youngest child of his father's fourth wife. The Gandhis belonged to the Bania subcaste of the Vaisya or farmers' and traders' caste. The name Gandhi in fact means grocer, but Gandhi's father, like his father before him, held the position of *diwan* or prime minister in the court of the prince of Porbandar, a small city state on the coast in the Gujarat region north of Bombay.

Gandhi's father, Karamchand, was a shrewd politician known above all for his loyalty and impartiality. He had a reputation as a skilful arbitrator in disputes and perhaps set an example for his son. Negotiating agreements between conflicting parties was the primary goal of Gandhi's own legal and political career.

Gandhi loved and respected his father but was even closer to his mother, Putlibai, who impressed

Gandhi as he appeared during his days in London as a law student. He is wearing the official clothing then required of students at the Inner Temple Law School: wing collar, bow tie, well-pressed white shirt, waistcoat and black jacket.

Gandhi (right) with his brother, Laxmidas, in 1886. Laxmidas, six years older than Mohandas, spent his whole working life in a succession of undistinguished jobs in the princely court of Rajkot.

Behind the half-barred window in the centre of this building, Gandhi was born on October 2, 1869. According to Hindu astrology, Gandhi's birth date indicated that he would have to face many struggles and trials in his lifetime.

him, above all, with her saintliness. She practised great self-denial, giving herself willingly to the service of others and strictly observing periods of religious fasting. One year she would not touch food without seeing the sun first. In the monsoon season, Mohandas would race outside to try to catch sight of the sun between rain clouds for her. If the sun did not appear, she would shrug, smiling, and wait until the next day.

As a schoolboy in the city of Rajkot, where Karamchand Gandhi moved the family, Mohandas was extremely shy. He rushed to and from school, too nervous to talk to any of his classmates. Then change intruded on his life. At the age of 13 Mohandas married a pretty, strong-willed girl his own age named Kasturbai.

This seems extraordinary young, but child marriages were a traditional Hindu custom. Parents arranged their children's marriages, often when the children were little more than infants. Love matches were almost unknown. As an adult Gandhi disapproved of child marriages, even though his own lasted 62 years. Just because the practice was an ancient tradition was no reason to continue it, thought Gandhi.

At first, marriage meant nothing more to Mohandas than elegant clothes, lavish dinners and processions, and someone new to play with. Soon, however, he was trying to assert a husband's traditional authority. He refused to let Kasturbai go out without his permission. She went out anyway. He tormented himself with jealousy. They would end up not speaking to each other. He tried to teach her to read at night but their lessons never got very far. Luckily, they did not spend more than half of their first five years of marriage together, since it was customary for the young wife to return to her father's house part of the time.

Mohandas was ashamed that he suffered fears that didn't bother Kasturbai, especially his fear of sleeping in the dark. In addition, he was small and not very strong. Sheik Mehtab, a confident and athletic older boy who fascinated Mohandas, played on these fears in order to convince Mohandas to eat meat. Like many Hindus, the Gandhis were vegetarians for religious reasons. Sheik Mehtab pointed to himself as an example of what meat-eating could do. Then he launched another argument: the Indians were a small, weak people because they didn't eat meat, and this was why the British, who did, had the strength to rule over them. If the Indians wanted to drive out the British, they would have to start eating meat.

Persuaded that it was his patriotic duty to become a meat-eater, Mohandas agreed to try, but a

Shown here is the interior of the house in Rajkot where Gandhi spent his childhood. Gandhi often said that he did not enjoy his schooldays. His school records indicate that he was an unpredictable student, sometimes showing brilliance, at other times exhibiting mediocrity.

combination of nerves and taste made him sick to his stomach the first time. Still, out of duty, he persisted and even grew to like the taste, but guilt at deceiving his parents eventually overcame him. He decided to postpone eating meat until he could do so openly, without risking parental disapproval.

It was only later that Gandhi became a vegetarian by choice, and as a boy, this was not the only aspect of traditional Hinduism that he questioned. He could not understand why contact with untouchables should mean pollution. He stopped going to the temple. At the same time, while he went so far as to question the existence of God, his belief in a moral code rooted in truth only grew stronger. Seeking truth became his goal.

One incident gave Mohandas his first lesson in nonviolence, the principle that would shape his adult life. Mohandas had stolen some gold from home. In shame he wrote a confession and handed it to his father. Reading it, Gandhi's father cried, and then embraced him. Truthful repentance had the power to inspire forgiveness instead of angry punishment.

Karamchand Gandhi died when his son was 17, after being bedridden with illness for two years. To his dismay Mohandas had left the bedside and run off to be with Kasturbai moments before his father's death.

Mohandas was the one whom his father and family had hoped would follow in the career of *diwan*. After an unsuccessful first term at college, a friend of the family suggested an alternative to Mohandas: why not study in England? A law degree would only take three years. And he would have the prestige of a British degree, too. His mother, however, worried that he would be corrupted by loose European society. Relenting, she gave her permission, only after Mohandas had sworn three vows: not to touch meat, alcohol or women.

There was still another block to his plans. The head of the Bania subcaste to which the Gandhis belonged tried to forbid Mohandas to leave. It was not possible to practise their religion properly in England. No Bania member had ever gone. Gandhi

Behold the mighty Englishman,
He rules the Indian small,
Because being a meat-eater
He is five cubits tall.

—Indian schoolboys' rhyme.

An aerial view of London's Trafalgar Square and White-hall, the nerve centre of the British empire.

replied that he did not believe it was against their religion to go overseas and he did not think the caste should interfere. It was the reply of someone unwilling simply to conform to tradition or orders, the action of one guided by an inner sense of purpose even at the risk of being expelled from the caste.

Not yet 19, Mohandas Gandhi sailed for England in September 1888, leaving Kasturbai and his first son, Harilal, behind with his family.

3

The London Student

In London, Gandhi found himself disoriented by a foreign world. The people, their clothes, even their houses seemed strange. His knowledge of English was mostly restricted to the written word. But perhaps an even greater difficulty was his lack of knowledge of English social customs. This made him acutely self-conscious.

Gandhi's vegetarian vow was proving especially hard to keep, although he was not one to break a sworn pledge. First, there were practical problems. His landlady, who had probably never met a vegetarian before, did not know what to feed him other than oatmeal, vegetables, and bread. In the cheap restaurants where he tried eating, he was once again forced to fill up with bread. To add to this, a friend told him that if he didn't eat meat, he would never be able to fit into English society.

This only made Gandhi more anxious to acquire other skills that would help him become an English gentleman instead of a bewildered stranger. As a young man, Gandhi was eager to fit in and establish his social status, even though he would later reject these goals. In his first month in London, he became a stylish and fastidious dresser. He took dancing, French, and elocution lessons, and even tried the violin, hoping to learn to appreciate Western music, which was so unlike what he was used to.

England's King George V (centre) and his son Edward, Prince of Wales, tour a British military camp in 1917. Gandhi finally met King George in 1931, while attending a conference in London. They exchanged few words, since George was still angry at the Gandhi-inspired boycott of Prince Edward's 1921 visit to India.

London crowds greeting Gandhi during the 1931 Round Table Conference, at which he represented the Indian Nationals. Here in London, some forty years earlier, he had spent his difficult and lonely student years.

At last he found a vegetarian restaurant. Joyfully, he ate his first full meal since his arrival. Not only were there other vegetarians in London, Gandhi discovered, but a London Vegetarian Society. Talking to its members, Gandhi met people who had decided to become vegetarians for philosophical and ethical as well as health reasons. Vegetarianism now became a conscious choice for him, too— no longer just an obligation.

The Society gave him a cause—he wrote articles in support of vegetarianism—and introduced him to a community of similar-minded people. It was Society members who first introduced Gandhi to the *Bhagavad Gita*, an epic poem that is practically a sacred text or prayer book to Hindus. Gandhi was embarrassed to admit that he had never read it before, although later in life he would turn to it continually. He read the Old Testament but was bored by it. In the Gospels, however, he discovered the Sermon of the Mount. Jesus's doctrine of turning the other cheek, with its insistence on nonviolence, struck a deep chord within him.

At the same time, Gandhi was busy studying at London University. The law exams were known to be so easy that few students even bothered to read the assigned textbooks, but Gandhi worked diligently anyway. He was called to the bar on June 10, 1891. Just two days later he sailed for home, anxious to return, only to learn on arrival that his mother had died while he was still in England. His brother had held back the news, not wanting Gandhi to disrupt his studies.

On his return to India, Gandhi was made to realize that he had studied law but had not learned how to practise it. And although he might have a prestigious British degree, he did not have the knowledge of Indian law that a lawyer in India required. Worst of all, he lacked the ability to speak in public—a skill essential for lawyers. In fact, he had difficulty talking in front of any group of people. In his first court case, he was too overwhelmed even to open his mouth.

In addition, Gandhi began to see just how much influence and politicking counted. Yet his attempt

Modern civilization . . . is ensouled by the spirit of selfishness and materialism . . . and seeks to increase bodily comforts.

—GANDHI

A 1925 view of a street in the City of London's financial district, where the economic exploitation of the colonies was orchestrated throughout the British imperial period.

to put in a good word for his brother with a British official whom he had met in England was disastrous: Gandhi was rudely thrown out of the man's office. There was something else he had to take into account, too. The relations between British and Indians were very different in colonial India than in England.

Without good prospects in his own country, Gandhi took an offer from a local Muslim mercantile firm with branch headquarters in the British colony of South Africa. The firm needed someone with a knowledge of English language and law to represent them for a year. It would prove to be a new beginning.

4

From Lawyer to Leader

Gandhi was travelling by train through South Africa to Pretoria, where he was about to try a case. A white man entered the first-class compartment in which Gandhi was sitting, stared at him, and left. He returned with two officials who told Gandhi to go to the third-class car. Gandhi insisted that he had a first-class ticket. Indians were not supposed to travel first-class. When Gandhi refused to move, he was pushed off the train and his luggage dumped after him.

He spent that night in the unlit waiting room of the Maritzburg station, shivering from the cold but too afraid to ask the luggage attendant for his coat. Should he stay and fight for his rights, or should he give up and go back to India, or should he just swallow the insults and complete his legal case? He chose to stay and fight against race prejudice. It was a night that changed the course of his life.

As Gandhi continued on to Pretoria, he encountered still more trouble. He was forced to give up his stage coach seat and sit outside by the driver. At hotels he was told there were no vacancies. As an Indian he was called "coolie" and "sammie".

In South Africa Gandhi confronted legalized discrimination for the first time. Indians were not allowed on the streets after 9:00 p.m. They were forced into ghettos. They could not own land except

A Johannesburg policeman checks a black African's papers. Blacks are still treated as second-class citizens in South Africa. Their freedom of movement around the country and in the cities was heavily restricted under the terms of South Africa's notorious "pass" laws, finally abolished in 1986.

Gandhi sits with his employees outside his law offices in Johannesburg, South Africa, in 1913. The woman on the right in Sonja Schlesin, a stenographer who applied for a job in Gandhi's office because she admired his ideals. Gandhi, in turn, greatly admired Sonja, calling her "the jewel of my house".

in restricted areas and had great difficulty obtaining business licences. People had to pay an annual residence tax simply because they were Indian. Even today South Africa is a country with a policy of legalized discrimination and segregation, called *apartheid,* against "coloureds", as all non-whites are labelled. Many nations have cut off relations with South Africa because they object to this practice.

South Africa was originally colonized by the Dutch in the 17th century. When the British took

> *Everybody seems to start with the assumption that the nonviolent method must be set down as a failure unless he himself at least lives to enjoy the success thereof.*
>
> —GANDHI

control over the southern territories of Natal and Cape Colony, the Dutch, who were called Boers, moved north to found the territories of Transvaal and the Orange Free State. The Indian community in South Africa was divided between free Indians and indentured labourers, who were still not as badly off as blacks. Gandhi's fight against discrimination, however, concentrated on his own people, who found their rights being taken away from them, and not on the plight of the black natives.

Indentured Indian labourers were brought over to

> *Civil disobedience is not a state of lawlessness and licence but presupposes a law-abiding spirit combined with self-restraint.*
> —GANDHI

Pimville, a black ghetto in Johannesburg, South Africa. Many of the hovels in this recent photograph date back to 1905, when Gandhi was dividing his time between the Phoenix Farm community and his Johannesburg law offices.

work for very low wages on five-year contracts. Between 1860 and 1890, 40,000 arrived. In spite of the hard conditions, they often chose to stay, instead of returning to poverty and starvation in India, even though they had to pay an annual tax to do so. The free Indians, many of whom were professionals or businessmen, established themselves in cities where they were becoming wealthy and successful. They were also becoming unwanted competition for the white community.

When Gandhi arrived in Pretoria he immediately sent a letter of protest to the railway company. Now, burning with urgency of his cause, he was no longer too frightened to speak in public. Yet, strangely, his emphasis was not on protest but self-improvement. Indians must combat the accusations made against them on the grounds of their way of life by proving the charges false. They must be as sanitary as possible, learn English (he offered to teach them), and cooperate with each other. Hindus and Muslims must forget their differences.

Meanwhile, Gandhi concluded his legal case by bringing the two contesting parties to an agreeable compromise. A lawyer's job, he realized, does not in fact depend on his eloquence in the courtroom but on gathering evidence. The true function of a lawyer is not to fight for one side but to search out the facts and negotiate a solution in the best interest of both sides. Gandhi would use his 20 years as a lawyer to put this belief into practice.

At a farewell party prior to his return to India, Gandhi happened to glance at the paper and noticed a proposed bill depriving Indians in Natal of the vote—yet another move to restrict their rights. He agreed to postpone his return and sent a petition with signatures to the Natal newspapers and the prime minister, who delayed the bill's passage by two days. Gandhi sent a second petition with 10,000 signatures to London newspapers and the London Colonial Office, which ruled against the bill. In response, the Natal Assembly simply passed a similar bill that did not mention Indians by name. Gandhi stayed on.

A hostel under construction in Johannesburg, South Africa, in 1972. Part of a project intended to house 60,000 unmarried blacks, such planning reflects the continuing oppression of non-whites in South Africa 60 years after Gandhi's departure.

5

Further Transformations

In 1894 Gandhi founded the Natal Indian Congress based on the model of the National Congress in India, started in 1885. The Congress was not a governing body of elected officials like the American Congress but a political party—even though members had no voting rights. It gave Gandhi a way to organize the Indian community. As in Pretoria, he once again urged self-improvement in three key areas: sanitation, education, and cooperation. Gandhi also recognized the important propaganda role the press could play in his campaign, and he used newspapers to call attention to the Indian movement, to defend against accusations, and to keep the public in England and India, as well as South Africa, informed of the current situation. When an indentured labourer beaten by his master came to Gandhi for help, Gandhi took up the cause of labourers as well. He defended their rights and fought to lower the tax they had to pay in order to stay on as free workers.

When Gandhi returned to India in 1896 to bring back Kasturbai and his two sons, he held public meetings about conditions in South Africa and even wrote a pamphlet describing them. Exaggerated reports of his activities in the South African press infuriated the white community there. In addition, they heard a rumour that he was return-

A monument in Johannesburg, South Africa, erected in 1913 to the memory of the 26,000 Boer women and children who died in the British concentration camps during the war. The victims were dependants of the rebel Boer farmers who had left their holdings to fight the British.

British troops march through Jamestown, South Africa, during the Boer War (1899-1902). Gandhi, although constantly worried by the limited civil rights of Indians in British-ruled South Africa, sincerely believed that the British empire was a force of good.

39

Lord Kitchener, the British commander-in-chief in South Africa from 1900 to 1902 and in India from 1902 to 1909. Many historians consider Kitchener to have been Britain's most memorable imperialist.

ing along with a boat filled with Indian immigrants.

Authorities refused to let the two boats dock for three weeks. When Gandhi stepped ashore, he was met by an angry mob who snatched away his turban and pelted him with rotten eggs, stones, and bricks. He was rescued by the wife of the police chief who shielded him with her umbrella. But when he was taken to the home of a friend to recover, the mob followed. Gandhi escaped disguised as an Indian police constable, with a scarf wrapped around a plate to serve as a helmet. Two white detectives accompanied him, with their faces painted to make them look like Indians.

To everyone's amazement, Gandhi refused to press charges against his attackers. Instead he once again turned to the press and gave an interview defending himself. The newspapers declared him unjustly accused and the rest of the white community had to agree.

In 1899, the Boer War broke out. Boers in the Transvaal wanted to repossess their gold mines, now under British ownership, and force the British out of Natal. Again, Gandhi's response astonished everyone. He would support the British—not by fighting but by forming an Indian ambulance corps. At first the British refused his offer, but when Gandhi and his corps did enter the action, they won war medals as well as praise from the press.

Gandhi's position was unpopular with many Indians, however. They wanted to remain neutral. At this stage, Gandhi still believed in finding freedom under British rule. If you are going to demand the rights of a citizen, he argued, then it is also your duty to defend those rights.

Gandhi still believed that the way to be "civilized" was to dress and behave like a European. In spite of their complaints, he made Kasturbai and his sons use knives and forks and wear uncomfortable shoes and socks instead of sandals or going bare-footed. A "civilized" appearance would bring credit to the community and give him the influence he thought he required to serve his people best.

At the same time, Gandhi pursued his own self-help schemes that were decidedly at odds with his goal of conformity. He cut his own hair and washed his own laundry. He became interested in nursing, home remedies, and faddish diets. He even delivered his third son. Gandhi never valued consistency. Being consistent was not, he thought, the way to the truth. As he struggled between old and new values he was anything but consistent.

While he fought for indentured labourers and refused to take money for public service, he insisted that the Indian community provide him with enough legal work to assure a high standard of living. In fact, he became prominent and well-to-do. When he made up his mind to return to India in 1901, he was showered with expensive gifts. Instead of keeping them, he set up a public fund with the money. But Kasturbai did not want to give up the jewellery she had received. "It was for *my* service", Gandhi argued. "Dont I deserve something for serving you?" Kasturbai replied.

With his family Gandhi was decidedly authoritarian. He insisted that Kasturbai submit to him, the way a wife was traditionally supposed to. While he cared for his sons, he would not give them a professional education such as he had, but wanted them to follow the way of life he was struggling to achieve.

When Gandhi left for India, he promised to return to South Africa if his presence was needed. The struggle was not over yet, and less than two years later he was called back again.

The British victory in the Boer War did not lessen the discrimination against Indians, and the British government of the new Union of South Africa was more interested in reaching a peaceful settlement with the defeated Boers than in the minority issue. On his return, Gandhi set up a law office in Johannesburg, the capital of the Transvaal where the Indian situation was the most tense.

In 1903, Gandhi founded his own newspaper, *Indian Opinion*, to provide the Indian cause with its own voice in the press. The paper was having financial difficulties when Gandhi read a book by the 19th-century British essayist John Ruskin. It

Winston Churchill as a war correspondent during the Boer War (1899-1902). Churchill, who later became prime minister of Britain, was one of Gandhi's most outspoken opponents in the British government during the 1930s and 1940s.

influenced him deeply and inspired him with an immediate solution. Ruskin stressed the equal value of all work and above all the dignity of manual labour. With these ideas in mind, Gandhi set up a self-supporting community in the country called the Phoenix Farm and moved the newspaper there.

The transformations in Gandhi's lifestyle and philosophy were becoming more extreme. He was increasingly intent on devoting himself to the service of others. A true life of service, he came to believe, required that he give up all possessions. Even his body should only exist to serve others and not be pampered with comforts. He restricted his diet to uncooked foods and began to engage in fasts. Stripping his life of possessions and training his mind to give things up willingly was at first a slow and painful process. Gandhi turned to the *Bhagavad Gita*, which he had first discovered in London, and which he interpreted in his own way as a plea for nonpossession. It became his guide for conduct.

A life of service also demanded a willingness to do the most degrading jobs, like cleaning out chamber pots. Gandhi seemed to take particular pleasure in performing such duties, and even went out of his

The principles that Gandhi derived from Ruskin:

1. That the good of the individual is contained in the good of all.

2. That the lawyer's work has the same value as a barber's, inasmuch as all have the same right of earning their livelihoods from their work.

3. That a life of labour—the life of the tiller of the soil and the handicraftsman—is the life worth living.

John Ruskin, a British essayist of the 19th century whose views on work deeply influenced Gandhi.

way to do them, as if he had to prove to himself that he could. He made Kasturbai follow his example: not only was she to clean out chamber pots but do so cheerfully. When she cried and told him she'd had enough, he angrily pushed her out of the house. Ashamed, he realized how much he had to learn to control his emotions as well.

In order to give himself over completely to public service, Gandhi felt he could no longer fully keep up his responsibilities to his family. Ties to wife and children interfered with a life devoted to service, he told himself, and were incompatible with his belief in practising absolute self-restraint, which meant giving up all his desires as well as possessions. True service would require both poverty and celibacy. In 1906, at the age of 37, Gandhi took a vow to abstain from sexual relations. He saw the vow, which he kept for the rest of his life, as a way of freeing himself. Did he also enjoy the difficulty involved in complete self-restraint? He told Kasturbai of his plan only after he had come to his decision. Although they no longer slept together, they continued to live and work together until Kasturbai's death.

Boers prepare to repel a British attack during the Boer War. The Boers were a people of Dutch descent whose humiliation of foreigners, including the British, during the 19th century led to war in 1899.

6

Satyagraha in South Africa

Gandhi's years in South Africa are often seen as just a preview to his struggle in India. In fact, he spent 20 years in South Africa, and it was here that his idea of *Satyagraha,* or nonviolent resistance, developed from a personal philosophy into a means of political protest and a way of organizing a mass movement. Gandhi would then go on to use these methods powerfully in India. Unfortunately, his struggle in South Africa did not have the same long-term effects as in India.

In 1906 the Transvaal government announced a bill that would require all Indians to register with the government, be fingerprinted, and carry a certificate of registration at all times. Indians could be asked to produce their certificates at any point, and the police could even enter homes to inspect them. This was a denial of the most basic civil rights. Gandhi was horrified.

He called a meeting in a Johannesburg theatre. Thousands of Indians came. They must be prepared to resist registration, Gandhi told them. Would they all have the strength when the time came, he wondered. One of the other speakers declared that he would swear in God's name to resist. As always, Gandhi took the idea of an oath very seriously. He stood up and warned people that swearing a vow

General Jan Smuts, the South African minister in charge of Indian affairs with whom Gandhi clashed repeatedly between 1906 and 1914. Smuts, a Boer by birth, who had fought the British during the Boer War, grew to admire Gandhi despite their constant political confrontations.

Gandhi poses with his wife, Kasturbai, shortly after their return to India from South Africa in 1915. Apart from occasional brief return visits, he had been away from India for 28 years by this time, and at first found it extremely difficult to readjust.

was not to be done lightly. They must be prepared to face threats, beatings, even imprisonment. Only if they believed they had the inner strength to be true should they swear. Then he encouraged them. Even if there were no more than a few true to their oath, they would bring victory. The entire audience rose and swore to resist.

How were they to resist? They would all simply refuse to obey the unjust law, and if harassed, refuse to respond with violence.

While Gandhi had a strategy, he still needed a name for it. He chose *Satyagraha*, "the force of truth and love". In Gandhi's native language, Gujarati, *satya* means truth and love, and *graha* means firmness. He did not like the term passive resistance, since passive suggests weakness and *Satyagraha* requires great inner strength. Later he would also use the term civil disobedience, after reading the *Essay on Civil Disobedience* by the 19th-century American, Henry David Thoreau, who believed that every person has the right to resist a governments's injustice.

In 1907 the Asiatic Registration Act was passed. Gandhi announced his plans for resistance in his paper, *Indian Opinion*. When he and his initial followers were sentenced to two months in prison, the movement only grew stronger, and jails continued to fill up. Gandhi's policy as a *Satyagrahi*, or someone who practises *Satyagraha*, was not only to refrain from violence but also to be courteous to and think well of opponents, officials, and gaolers. This he said, could be the hardest part of *Satyagraha*. They were not fighting against individuals, however, only against the evils of the system.

Seeing that imprisoning their leader was not stopping the resisters, General Smuts, the minister in charge of Indian affairs, offered Gandhi a compromise: if the Indians registered voluntarily, Smuts would release those in prison and repeal the act. Gandhi agreed.

His move confused and angered many. Did he believe Smuts' promise? A *Satyagrahi* is not afraid to trust his opponent, Gandhi said. He himself was the first to register, even when he was attacked by a

> *To see the universal and all-pervading Spirit of Truth face to face one must be able to love the meanest creatures as oneself. And a man who aspires after that cannot afford to keep out of any field of life. That is why my devotion to Truth has drawn me into the field of politics and ... those who say that religion has nothing to do with politics do not know what religion means.*
>
> —GANDHI

The Empire Theatre in Johannesburg, where on September 11, 1906, Gandhi addressed a meeting of Indians protesting against the Transvaal government's Asiatic Registration Act.

fellow Indian on the way to the registration office.

When Smuts did not repeal the act, as many Indians had feared, Gandhi and 2,000 followers burned their certificates in a huge bonfire. A British news correspondent compared the burning to the Boston Tea Party. The *Satyagrahis* continued their resistance, and some served up to five jail terms in succession.

Finding a way to support the families of imprisoned *Satyagrahis* became a problem. A German friend and follower of Gandhi bought land and gave it to the movement. Once again, Gandhi set up a communal farm, where members grew their own food, ate no meat, engaged in manual labour, and made their own furniture. Gandhi named the farm

47

after the Russian novelist, Leo Tolstoy, the author of *War and Peace,* who later in life became deeply religious and, like Gandhi, gave up his possessions, refrained from violence, and devoted himself to manual labour.

In 1913 a Supreme Court decision ruled that only Christian marriages registered with the government were considered legal. With this, Indian wives were deprived of their status and their children became officially illegitimate. The ruling brought women into the resistance movement. Kasturbai insisted on being allowed to participate, even though Gandhi did not actively encourage her.

The first group of 16 women protesters from Phoenix Farm was arrested. Gandhi sent a second group of women from Tolstoy Farm to the coal mines in Natal where they urged the miners to strike in protest. This was the first strike by non-whites in South Africa.

When the mining company countered by turning off the electricity and water in the housing compound, Gandhi urged the 6,000 jobless, moneyless miners to march with him from Natal into the Transvaal. Either they would be put in prison, where at least they would be fed, or they would go on to Tolstoy Farm. Only Gandhi was arrested, and locked, with handcuffs, in an unlit cell about three metres (ten feet) long. The miners were sent back to Natal and violently forced back to work.

Reports of the march, further sympathy strikes, and the South African government's harsh response drew outrage and pressure from Britain. The viceroy in India demanded a commission to investigate the treatment of Indians. General Smuts released Gandhi and set up a commission—but no Indians, or even anyone pro-Indian was on it, and one member was known to be anti-Indian.

Labelling the commission a hoax, Gandhi called for a mass protest march. He cancelled the protest, however, when white railway workers all across South Africa went on strike, crippling the country and threatening to topple the government. He did not want to mix these separate issues, he said, and he certainly did not believe in taking any form of advantage of an opponent at a time of weakness.

Impressed by Gandhi's move, Smuts called him to his office to talk. In this atmosphere of reconciliation they reached an agreement, which became the Indian Relief Act in June 1914. It was, in fact, a compromise. Indians were not granted full rights, although non-Christian marriages were legalized, and the tax on former indentured labourers was abolished. Yet Gandhi saw the outcome as a victory that showed how effective *Satyagraha* could be as political tool.

Two weeks later, Gandhi left South Africa for good. Smuts, who later expressed his deep respect for Gandhi and his humane methods, was no doubt glad to see the troublemaker go.

Caste has nothing to do with religion in general and Hinduism in particular. It is a sin to believe anyone else is inferior or superior to ourselves.
—GANDHI

Russian author Leo Tolstoy in 1908. Gandhi greatly admired Tolstoy's philosophy of humility and self-sufficiency, and in 1909 wrote him an account of the Indian noncooperation movement in South Africa.

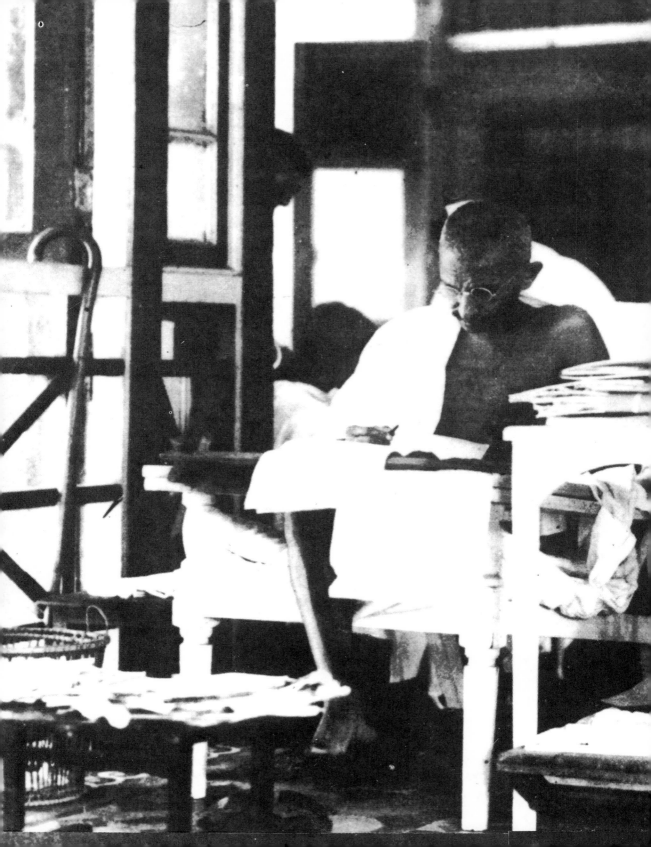

7

Turmoil in India

Just after Gandhi left South Africa, World War I broke out. His support, once again, of Britain, India's oppressor, and his cooperation attitude towards the war, in contradiction of his nonviolent principles, troubled many Indians. Gandhi was a hero to Indian nationalists even before his return. His people knew him as the defender of Indian rights against discrimination in South Africa and as a believer in nonviolent resistance. They knew him, too, as a supporter of Indian self-government and as the author of a pamphlet called *Hind Swaraj* or "Home Rule". In it Gandhi outlined a vision of Indian self-rule which included keeping up close ties with Britain. He did not want India to free itself from British power only to copy a British-style government, however. Why assume the Western model was the best? Instead, he envisioned a complete reform of Indian society. The modern, industrialized civilization that British rule brought to India had only served to weaken the country politically and economically.

Gandhi arrived in Bombay in January 1915. Rather than fighting for a cause from the start, he took the advice of G. K. Gokhale, an older states-man and nationalist leader who saw gandhi as his political successor. Gokhale undertook to be Gan-

India's princely states enjoyed largely independent status, and were not directly under British administration. Here, in 1931, the Maharajah (prince) of the state of Mysore rides his elephant before leaving his palace to participate in a religious procession.

Gandhi attends to correspondence at a seaside resort near Bombay in 1924, while recovering from a prison term to which he was sentenced in 1922 for organizing a mass civil disobedience campaign.

British troops evacuate their wounded from a battlefield in France during World War I. Gandhi, in London for a few months at the beginning of the war, organized Indian volunteers for service in the British army's Field Ambulance Corps until poor health forced him to return to India in 1915.

dhi's mentor, but died just months after Gandhi's return. "Spend your first year with your ears open", Gokhale had said, "and your mouth shut."

In order to reacquaint himself with his own country, Gandhi travelled across India in filthy, jam-packed third-class railway cars, wearing only a cheap cloth cap and a *dhoti*, or peasant's long loincloth. Everywhere, politicians showered attention on him and peasants crowded to see the great man. Was this the hero they expected? No doubt they were taken aback by his appearance. He was small and scrawny. When he spoke to crowds his voice was weak and, in these days before loudspeakers, often impossible to hear.

Needing somewhere to settle down, Gandhi founded Sabamarti *ashram* in his native region of Gujarat with money donated by textile manufacturers in the nearby capital of Ahmedabad. Traditionally an *ashram* is a retreat for the religious. Gandhi's *ashram* was a self-supporting community like Phoenix and Tolstoy Farms. All the residents swore to be true to the same principles as Gandhi and, like him, renounced meat, sex, and alcohol.

Although residents had pledged to be against "untouchability", the arrival of an untouchable family brought conflict. Some members left the community. The owner of the *ashram's* land would

These ruins at Verdun, France, testify to the ferocity of the fighting during World War I. Although India's princely states had sent troops to fight with the Allies, losses were so immense that in 1918 Britain appealed for men from the rest of India. Gandhi, although opposed to violence, loyally aided the recruitment programme.

> *To prepare for home rule, individuals must cultivate the spirit of service, renunciation, truth, nonviolence, self-restraint, patience.*
>
> —GANDHI

> *Political self-government... is no better than individual self-government and therefore is to be attained by precisely the same means that are required for individual self-government or self-rule.*
>
> —GANDHI

not allow ashramites to use the well. Financial sponsors backed out. The collective was on the brink of shutting down, when out of the blue a wealthy stranger drove up in his car, handed Gandhi enough money to support the *ashram* for a year, and drove off.

Ashram residents called Gandhi *"Bapu"*, which means father, and the name stuck. It was not long before Rabindranath Tagore, the Nobel prize-winning Indian poet, described him as "The Great Soul in Peasant's Garb". Soon Gandhi heard voices calling *"Mahatma"*,or Great Soul, wherever he went.

It was in 1916. Gandhi's year was up and he was ready to "speak". Dressed in white homespun, Gandhi stood on the speaker's platform at the opening ceremonies of the Hindu University, sur-rounded by British officials in uniforms decked with medals, and native princes and princesses, glittering with jewels. He began by apologizing for talking in English, then addressed the issue of self-rule. First we have to make ourselves *fit* for self-government, he said. He described India's poverty. Educated Indians should be ready to serve the poor, who were the real base of India's political power. Turning to his audience, he urged them to strip off their jewels and finery. The shouting became so loud that he was forced to break off. Gandi's idea of independence was obviously not what others had in mind. India's weakness was not due to the British alone. An independent Indian government would in fact have no effect on the poor and uneducated who made up 80 percent of India's population. The country had to be strengthened from within before it could win freedom. Nationwide self-reliance had to come before self-rule.

Gandhi soon found an opportunity to show that India's poor had political power. After a peasant worker begged persistently for his help, Gandhi went with him to Champaran, a region in the Himalayan foothills. There, Indian workers who had previously paid a share of their crops as rent to their British landowners were now not only forced to pay in money but faced large rent increases they

A British fort dominates the landscape in India's North-West region, near the border with Afghanistan. Britain maintained control of Afghanistan at substantial military cost throughout the 19th century, using it as a buffer state between India and the other major power in the region, Russia.

could not afford. When Gandhi began to gather evidence for the case, local authorities ordered him to leave. He stayed, only to be arrested. Angry crowds gathered outside the courthouse in protest. Yes, Gandhi said, he was prepared to accept the penalty for disobeying the law. Fearing the response of the local peasants if they pressed charges, the authorities released him, and Gandhi continued to interview workers for evidence. A government decision compelled the landlords to lower their rents.

Gandhi saw events in Champaran as a victory. Not only had he shown the poor that they could take action to help themselves, but the court case demonstrated that the British government could not order him around in his own country.

Back in Ahmedabad, Gandhi was called in to arbitrate a wage dispute between mill owners and workers. Both sides respected him. In fact, some of the mill owners were sponsors of Gandhi's *ashram.*

An Indian army cavalry
unit patrols India's Peshawar province in 1932.
There were two major military forces in India during
the colonial period—
British regular troops and
the Indian army, which
was recruited in India and
led by British officers. Indian army units fought
with great distinction in
Africa and the Middle East
during World War II.

When an impatient group of workers walked off the job, however, the owners backed out of the negotiations. While careful to keep in close touch with the owners, Gandhi counselled the strikers. He told them not to demand too much and outlined the way they should conduct a nonviolent strike. They pledged to follow his guidelines. *"Ek Tek"*, or "keep the pledge", became their strike motto.

After two weeks of the strike, morale dropped. Without money to buy food, the workers wanted to return to work. It was all very well for Gandhi to tell them to hold out, but he was not stuck in their position.

Troubled, Gandhi was struggling to decide what to do when an idea struck him. He announced to the workers that he would fast in their support. We should fast, not you, they said in concern. What matters is that you keep your pledge, Gandhi told them.

This was Gandhi's first public fast to support a cause he believed in. He would continue to fast in moments of political crisis throughout his life. Gandhi did not consider fasting to be blackmail but a way of bringing the other party to see what he felt was right and agreeing voluntarily with him. If he was fasting in a wrong cause, then only he and no one else would suffer for it. You should only fast to help those you care for, he said, and only when you feel helpless to do anything else. You could not force an enemy to change by fasting. A fast is also a dramatic gesture, and drama never lost its appeal for Gandhi.

Inevitably, though, a fast works on other people by putting pressure on them to act—not necessarily because they come to share your point of view but because they don't want to be responsible for your death. The mill owners felt under pressure and quickly agreed to a pay raise.

Gandhi continued to assume hopefully that Britain would grant India self-government after the war and that loyalty to Britain would be met by fair treatment in return. One and a half million Indians fought on the British side in World War I, and when Gandhi was asked to recruit more, he agreed. Why?

> *I hold it to be a virtue to be disaffected towards a government which in its totality has done more harm to India than any previous system.*
> —GANDHI

> *Those who live in England, far away from the East, have now got to realize that Europe has completely lost her former moral prestige in Asia. She is no longer regarded as the champion throughout the world of fair dealing, and the exponent of high principle, but as the upholder of Western race supremacy and the exploiter of those outside her own borders.*
> —RABINDRANATH TAGORE

> *There could be no question of undue severity... I thought I would be doing a jolly lot of good.*
> —GENERAL DYER

If people are not strong enough to stay out of the war, then they should take part in order to end the war, he rationalized. It was a position he would later reject.

The response of the Indian people was far from enthusiastic. Trudging from village to village, Gandhi caught dysentery. He was near death when Kasturbai persuaded him to drink goat's milk, even though he had sworn to abstain from milk. "Only from cow's milk", she argued, and weakly he agreed. Her act may well have saved his life.

Throughout India, the Home Rule movement was growing and along with it anti-British feelings. Although fought in Europe, the war resulted in food shortages, soaring prices, and strikes in India. Anger mounted. In concern, the government imprisoned the Home Rule leaders, restricted the rights of free speech, and censored the press. When the war ended, the restrictions were not repealed. The Rowlatt Commission sent from Britain in 1919 advised their extension and, since India was so unsettled, stated that independence should not even be reconsidered for another ten years.

Gandhi, once hopeful, was now outraged. He searched for a way to respond. While he wanted a countrywide demonstration, he also wanted to make sure that it could be kept under control. To add to the difficulty, this time he was not protesting against one specific bill as with the registration act in South Africa.

He announced a one-day, nationwide *hartal,*or strike. People were not just to stop work but Indians of all religions were to join together in fasting and prayer. On April 6, 1919, from villages to cities, the country shut down. Demonstrators marched in the streets. Elsewhere, violence disrupted the supposedly peaceful *hartal.* Rioters blocked trains, destroyed railway stations, looted stores, and burned government offices. The people were not ready for *Satyagraha,* Gandhi realized. They lacked the self-restraint it required. He called off the resistance campaign.

In the city of Amritsar, which had been shaken after the *hartal* by riots and attacks between

British and Indians, General Dyer of the British army was called in to take charge of the situation. Dyer banned all public gatherings among Indians. He made only a few, not widely heard, announcements of the ban, however. When the Indian community held a meeting the next day in a large, enclosed courtyard, Dyer made no move to cancel it. Instead, he and his men blocked the exits to the courtyard and fired into the crowd until they ran out of ammunition. Nearly 400 people were killed and 1,200 lay wounded. No one could rescue them until after the curfew was lifted the next day. Nor did Dyer's work end there. His men shot at an Indian funeral to disperse it. Indians were forced to crawl past the site where a British schoolteacher had been assaulted.

Although Dyer was reprimanded by the army, he was never punished. In response to an investigation of the massacre, Dyer said that he had not wanted simply to disperse the crowd but to produce "sufficient moral effect". His attitude embodied the worst extremes of British imperialism. With this atrocity, Gandhi's faith in the British empire was shattered.

A British armoured reconnaissance unit patrols India's North-West Frontier in 1930. The British military presence in India was substantial throughout the colonial period, and readily available for the suppression of protests and other disturbances.

8

Noncooperation

B_y 1920 Gandhi had put a new method of resistance into action: noncooperation. Independence from Britain was his goal. Noncooperation was Gandhi's term for a boycott of everything British — law courts, jobs, schools, clothing. He saw it as an effective way to attract world attention to the Indian cause at the same time.

By 1920 Gandhi was also the undisputed leader if the Indian National Congress, the nationalist political party. Dominated by upper-middle-class, English-educated Indians, the Congress Party was troubled by caste and religious differences. It met once a year and passed numerous resolutions but failed to inspire much action.

As its leader, Gandhi took the opportunity to reorganize the party, guided by his belief that India's political leaders had to be put in touch with the mass of India's people. Meetings were to be held throughout the year. Membership was opened up to the lower classes. Muslims and those from small towns and villages were encouraged to join. These changes were, in fact, to Gandhi's advantage, since he drew on the support of the new lower-class representatives to pass a series of resolutions endorsing *Satyagraha* as the means to freedom and recommending full participation in noncooper-

Gandhi and his followers conduct a spinning demonstration in an untouchable village, April 1946.

Jawaharlal Nehru is embraced by his mother in 1889. Nehru, a leading figure in the independence movement, was one of Gandhi's most prominent political disciples and became the first prime minister of India in 1947.

Indian government employees, stripped to their underwear, march through New Delhi, India, in 1983. They are demanding new synthetic cloth uniforms instead of old-fashioned cotton garments. Gandhi's vision of a homespun future for Indian textiles did not survive independence, as India industrialized rapidly after 1947.

Nehru poses in the uniform of the Officer Training Corps at England's Cambridge University in 1906. Most leading members of the Indian National Congress were wealthy and English-educated.

ation. The old, upper-class leaders of Congress felt threatened by noncooperation since it meant they would have to give up their professional jobs and their substantial incomes. If we stick to nonviolent noncooperation, Gandhi told them all, India will have home rule within a year.

Gandhi was still unsure if the people were ready for *Satyagraha*, or if they understood exactly what he was asking of them. Nor did he know if they really believed in nonviolence except in so far as it was useful to them. The Indian people were in need of a leader, and Gandhi had taken up their cause—self-rule. They would follow him because he was *Mahatma*, a holy man whom many believed to have mystical powers. The nonviolence that he preached made practical sense simply because they did not have the means to mount an armed rebellion.

With political skill, Gandhi had succeeded in aligning the people's cause with his beliefs. Yet he sincerely wanted to be understood, not just blindly worshipped as he so often was. His legs were often covered with scratches from people trying to touch him. "Though a noncooperator", he once joked, "I should gladly subscribe to a bill to make it criminal for anybody to call me *Mahatma* and touch my feet." In order to educate people for *Satyagraha*, he set up a Volunteer Corps. Among its members was Jawaharlal Nehru, the future Congress leader and prime minister of India.

Gandhi planned the noncooperation campaign in careful stages in an attempt to prevent a collapse into widespread disorder. Indian counterparts to British institutions were established. The boycott of British textiles, which dominated the Indian market, was to take place alongside a revival of handspinning and the wearing of homespun clothing.

Most educated Indians did not agree with Gandhi's resistance to industrialization and his wholehearted support of handspinning. Gandhi argued that spinning was a way for India's millions of agricultural poor, who spent much of their year in idleness anyway, to add to their meagre incomes. Before the British came, spinning had had its place in most homes. India certainly did not need labour-saving devices. White homespun cotton became the Congress Party uniform. Gandhi stripped himself of his British-made cloak and turban, and wore nothing but a loincloth, the uniform of the poorest of India's poor.

At first, the government thought little of non-

I had to disobey the British law because I was acting in obedience with a higher law, with the voice of my conscience.
—GANDHI

Nehru and his father, Motilal, in 1925. For many years a highly-paid lawyer, Motilal gave up his practice in 1920 to devote himself to Gandhi's independence movement. His imprisonment by the British in 1930 ruined his health and he died shortly after his release.

cooperation and did not even bother to interfere. Then it clamped down, imprisoning 30,000 people. Riots spread. Censorship came into force. Although a year was up, self-rule was nowhere in sight.

Gandhi was under pressure to take action. People were muttering that independence could not be won without force. Even though he feared that protesters might get out of control and break into revolt, Gandhi agreed to lead mass resistance, but planned to test *Satyagraha* in one region first. Before he could even begin, riots in another town ended in the bloody deaths of a squad of British policemen. In dismay Gandhi called off the whole *Satyagraha* campaign. His colleagues turned on him in anger. Why back down now? It is better to seem weak than to be so weak as to break our oath of nonviolence, he told them.

With Gandhi's popularity at an all-time low, the British government considered it a good time to arrest him without risking mass violence as a result. By putting him on trial, however, they only aided his cause. Gandhi spoke in his own defence to a packed courtroom. What was a crime in law, he saw as "the highest duty of a civilian". In response the judge declared that "it would be impossible to ignore the fact that you are in a different category from any person I have ever tried or am likely to try." Even Gandhi's political opponents admired him, the judge admitted. He sentenced Gandhi to six years, adding that he hoped the government would consider reducing the term.

Gandhi served only two years of his sentence, spending the time reading, spinning, and writing his autobiography, *The Story of My Experiments with the Truth*. In January 1924, he suffered a severe attack of appendicitis but refused medical assistance on religious grounds. The authorities, terrified of an uprising if he died while in their hands, pleaded with him to undergo an operation. Convinced that their fear was justified, he finally agreed. A month later they released him, although still anxious about the state of his health. Besides, they no longer saw a free Gandhi as much of a threat.

My resistance to Western civilization is really a resistance to its indiscriminate and thoughtless imitation based on the assumption that Asiatics are fit only to copy everything that comes from the West.
—GANDHI

Indian native police, led by their British officers, put down a demonstration in Bombay on July 30, 1930. The demonstrators are protesting against the arrest of Indian troops in Peshawar province who refused an order to charge a procession of Gandhi supporters.

Indians in Bombay walk past the debris which resulted from fighting between Muslims and Hindus in June 1932. Disputes between Hindu and Muslim political leaders so damaged the unity of the independence movement that even Gandhi failed to achieve a reconciliation.

Fighting breaks out between two factions of the untouchable caste in Bombay, July 1932. Some untouchables wanted the separate electoral status which the British eventually gave them, while others believed, as did Gandhi, that such legislation would condemn them to remaining a depressed class.

Gandhi stepped out into the world to dicover the nationalist movement in shambles and Congress split by infighting. Hindu and Muslim conflicts posed a serious threat. India's Muslims were growing convinced that they would suffer discrimination as a religious minority in a free India. Muslim political leaders refused to cooperate with Hindus. Riots provoked by religious strife spread through the country. Seeing this as his and India's most pressing concern, Gandhi announced that he would start a 21-day fast. Regardless of the British, there could be no home rule without Hindu and Muslim unity. In many ways a devout Hindu, Gandhi was a deeply religious man who believed strongly that people should tolerate and respect each others' different religions. All religions were ways to reach truth.

He made the shrewd choice to fast in the home of a Muslim friend, drinking only water with a little salt, while Hindu and Muslim leaders met anxiously for talks and the people demonstrated their unity in the streets. At the end of 21 days, with Hindus and Muslims gathered at his bedside, Gandhi sipped some orange juice to break his fast.

There was another serious problem in Gandhi's mind: untouchability. How can we complain of our treatment by the British when this is what we do to our own kind, he asked fellow Hindus. Withdrawing from the troubled political scene, he set out to bring his reforms to the villages first-hand. Gandhi travelled the country, staying in the homes of untouchables in order to break the taboo against them by his example. He also educated people in what he called his Constructive Programme. This consisted of three main goals: an end to untouchability, Hindu and Muslim unity, and the spinning and wearing of homespun cloth.

Spinning became virtually an obsession for Gandhi. He wanted all Indians to spin for at least half an hour a day as a kind of spiritual meditation and as a way of putting educated Indians who looked down on manual labour in touch with the millions who depended on it. Spinning would not only give dignity to manual labour but also represented Gandhi's ideal of independence—political, economic, and individual—through self-improvement. The spinning wheel became the symbol of Indian nationalism.

In 1927 the Congress Party was split in debate. Should it demand full independence or dominion status (the British monarch remaining constitutional head of state) such as Australia and Canada had? Should independence be immediate or gradual? Throughout the country, restlessness was mounting. In December 1928 the Congress Party called on Gandhi to guide them. If India did not even have dominion status within a year, he announced, he would lead the country into mass civil disobedience to achieve independence.

Margaret Sanger, the American authority on birth control whom Gandhi met in 1936. Their encounter distressed Gandhi, who believed sex was a sin unless intended to produce a child. After Gandhi's death the Indian government, fearing continuing overpopulation, officially encouraged birth control.

9

A Grain of Salt

The year was up. On December 31, 1929 Congress members, led by the new president, Jawaharlal Nehru, unfurled the flag of Indian independence. Then they waited for a signal from Gandhi to launch mass resistance. At Sabamarti *ashram* Gandhi waited in turn for an inner voice to tell him what to do.

In March he announced his plans both to India and the viceroy. With only a few followers, including Nehru, he set out on his Salt March. Soon thousands joined their 24-day trek to the coast and watched as Gandhi walked into the sea, prayed, then picked up a few grains of salt left by evaporated sea water on the shore. He had broken the law that made it illegal to obtain salt except through the British, who controlled all salt production. Soon the poor all along the coast were gathering sea water in pans and scraping away the salt left when the water dried. In the cities the wealthy competed with each other to buy Indian-made salt.

Gandhi's act, which at first had puzzled so many, proved to be a powerful nonviolent demonstration that India was impatient, and ready, for self-rule. Although the British still held on to India, they had suffered a significant moral and psychological defeat. After the Salt March, Indians no longer looked up to the British as a superior power or

> *My effort should never be to undermine another's faith but to make him a better follower of his own faith.*
> —GANDHI

Gandhi shortly before his arrest in January 1932.

Gandhi arrives in England for the Round Table Conference on Indian independence, September 12, 1931. To Gandhi's surprise, he was driven to London while his followers completed their journey by train. The British authorities kept Gandhi's visit low-key, fearing possible displays of public sympathy.

Followers of Gandhi hold a political rally on the beach at Madras, May 27, 1930. Gandhi had been arrested on May 5 for initiating the massive civil disobedience campaign which followed the Salt March.

An Indian army cavalryman charges into a crowd of nationalists in 1930. The demonstrators were preparing to raid a government salt deposit. The viceroy in India at the time, Lord Irwin, was a kindly man who disliked the harsh measures which the civil disobedience campaign forced him to take.

Rabindranath Tagore, the Indian poet, painter, and philosopher in November 1930. Gandhi's noncooperation campaign during 1920 disturbed Tagore, who approved of Gandhi's desire for Indian independence, but disliked the anti-Western aspects of Gandhi's teachings.

feared them. The freedom from fear was a major step towards political freedom.

In spite of mass arrests, and even after Gandhi himself was imprisoned without charges or trial, nonviolence prevailed. The planned raid on the Dharsana Salt Works that had led to Gandhi's arrest went on without him. Twenty-five hundred *Satyagrahis* marched towards the great salt pans that stood surrounded by ditches and barbed wire. Four hundred policemen armed with steel-covered clubs met them and struck down row after row of protesters. Those behind never faltered. Webb Miller, a reporter for United Press, recounted the horror to the Western world. "Not one of the marchers even raised an arm to fend off the blows...From where I stood I heard the sickening whack of the clubs on unprotected skulls."

It was hard for a Westerner, accustomed to seeing

Thousands of Hindus and Muslims gather by the Sabamarti river at Ahmedabad, India, in 1931 to hear Gandhi make a speech.

violence returned for violence, to understand this refusal to retaliate that Gandhi had instilled in India's people. His power was unlike anything Miller had ever witnessed. There was something deeply Eastern about Gandhi's methods. Could he have been who he was or done what he did anywhere other than India?

The gaols overflowed with more than 100,000 people. The country was at a standstill. The effects of noncooperation and boycotts took a serious economic toll. Realizing that holding India by force was doomed to failure, the British government began to face up to the idea of independence. In

1931 Gandhi and other Congress leaders were released, and after Gandhi's request for an interview, he and the viceroy, Lord Irwin, met for a series of eight talks. Still there were those in England opposed to Irwin's cooperative stance, among them Winston Churchill, who later became prime minister. He angrily described Gandhi as a "seditious lawyer . . . posing as a half-naked fakir", who had no right to negotiate with the British government.

In March Irwin and Gandhi reached an agreement, known as the Delhi Pact. Nonviolent resistance would be called to a halt in exchange for the release of the imprisoned protesters and the granting of salt rights—but without any promise of self-government, either in the form of dominion status or true independence. His colleagues criticized Gandhi's compromise. There is a point at which a *Satyagrahi* cannot refuse to negotiate with an opponent, he argued.

In August Gandhi left for London where the British government and the Indian representatives were to meet for discussion at the Round Table Conference. Gandhi caught the public eye and gained the sympathy of some British workers. He insisted on living in a London slum and visited the industrial Lancashire region to talk to textile workers who had lost jobs due to the Indian boycott of

British statesman and wartime prime minister Winston Churchill. In 1930 he severely criticized the viceroy in India, Lord Irwin, for allowing Indian independence leaders to confer with Gandhi while he was serving a prison term.

British cloth. Gandhi described India's poverty and its struggle for independence. "You have three million unemployed", he told them. "We have over 300 million unemployed." "If I was in India, I would say the same thing Mr. Gandhi is saying", one worker declared.

The conference, on the other hand, accomplished nothing, and discord between Hindus and Muslims divided the Indian delegates. Gandhi returned to India in despair only to find a new viceroy with a tough new policy. Congress leaders had been arrested and the Congress Party itself outlawed. When Gandhi called for civil disobedience in protest, he too found himself behind bars.

It was while Gandhi was in prison that the British government announced its proposal for a new modified Indian constitution that would include separate elections not only for Hindu and Muslim representatives, but also for untouchables. The separation of untouchables had been demanded by the untouchables' political leader, Bhimrao Ambedkar, who did not want untouchables to find themselves squeezed out of power by caste Hindus.

Gandhi saw any kind of segregation as dangerous. Even if separate elections guaranteed untouchables some rights, uniting Hindu society

> *Religions are different roads converging to the same point. What does it matter that we take different roads as long as we reach the same goal. In reality, there are as many different religions as there are individuals.*
>
> —GANDHI

As viceroy of India from 1925 to 1931, Lord Irwin showed much sympathy to the independence movement. A friend of Gandhi once payed tribute to Irwin's deep religious convictions, describing the Gandhi-Irwin conference of 1931 as a meeting between two Mahatmas.

Lord Irwin attends the Maharajah of the princely state of Kathurpala, India, in December 1927. Indian princes in Gandhi's time were descended from the princes who remained independent following the Indian Mutiny of 1857, at which time Britain installed a political administration in India.

was the essential thing. In fact, Gandhi wanted the whole caste system eliminated. In prison, Gandhi, now 63 years old, began a fast that would last until death or until Hindus and untouchables agreed to form a single political unit. In the seven days that his fast lasted Gandhi's health deteriorated rapidly. Outside the prison there were frantic negotiations between India and London to rework the proposed constitution. Although the actual changes were slight, the untouchables, the British, and Gandhi accepted them.

Ambedkar labelled Gandhi's fast "a stunt". Nehru considered it emotional and dramatic but not a valid political statement. Yet as the anxious days passed, Nehru had to admit that Gandhi was inspiring a wave of self-purification throughout the

Gandhi attends the Round Table Conference in September 1931. As one of 87 delegates from the princely states and British India, he was unable to exert as much influence as he had hoped, since all the other delegates had their own points to make.

country. Hindus stayed away from cinemas and restaurants, and even postponed weddings. Caste Hindus invited untouchables to eat with them. Temples and schools opened their doors to untouchables. While Gandhi could not wipe out the centuries-old taboo against untouchability, he did impress on people that it was morally wrong, which was something no law could do.

Gandhi continued to work for the untouchables' cause from prison. He founded a paper dedicated to this central social problem, which he called *Harijan.* This means "Children of God" and was the name Gandhi used to replace the demeaning term "untouchables". When Gandhi began another fast, fear of his death made the authorities release him, yet he persisted through the full 21 days and survived.

Once out of prison Gandhi continued to concentrate on social reform. In 1936, after closing down Sabamarti *ashram,* he founded a new community called Sevagram, which means "service village", where he lived for the rest of his life. Sevagram was located close to the goegraphic centre of India, which was also its poorest part, populated mostly by untouchables.

Gandhi's home was a small, mud-and-bamboo hut which contained a spinning wheel, a straw mat, a low writing table, and two shelves for books.

A massive crowd in Bombay listens to a speech by Gandhi on January 3, 1932. Gandhi, calling for renewed civil disobedience, was arrested later that day. The speed of the official reaction demonstrated that the new viceroy, Lord Willingdon, was a harsher disciplinarian than his predecessor, Lord Irwin.

A view of Gandhi's Sevagram *ashram*, near Wardha in central India. Located in an inhospitable area, infested with snakes and malaria, the village failed to remain as remote from civilization as Gandhi had hoped. Road and telephone communications linked Servagram to the outside world shortly after its foundation in April 1936.

His possessions amounted to little more than his simple clothing, two food bowls, fountain pens and paper, his glasses, and pocket watch. He slept little, rising every morning at 4:00 A.M. His meals consisted of fruit, nuts, and goat's milk. As inaccessible as Sevagram was, Gandhi could not stop people from all over India and around the world from making the trek to see him. He would talk to them about anything from politics to personal problems. He also kept up an enormous correspondence and wrote a steady stream of articles. To give himself a rest from his hectic schedule, Gandhi had a practice of keeping "silent Mondays", when he would not talk and communicated only through written notes.

Sevagram served as a model for the kind of self-sufficient cooperative community that Gandhi

Field Marshal Lord Birdwood inspects Indian soldiers in London in 1937, shortly before the coronation of King George VI of England. Birdwood had been military secretary to Lord Kitchener, the commander of British forces in South Africa during the Boer War (1899-1902).

Gandhi speaks at a civic reception in Calcutta in 1934. He visited the city to mediate a dispute between warring factions of India's National Congress.

wanted India's 700,000 villages to become. This was the heart of his vision of a new, free India. He educated people in reforms that covered everything from village government to keeping the water supply clean. He also wanted to stop the massive waves of migration to big cities that left millions stranded in slums. He believed in village self-rule just as he believed in individual self-rule. His kind of independence required both. Self-reliance and individualism were the keys to Gandhi's freedom. "I want freedom for full expression of my personality", he said. "I must be free to build a staircase to Sirius if I want to."

10
The Bitter Taste of Freedom

In September 1939 Britain entered World War II. Without consulting the Indians, the viceroy went ahead and declared India at war as well. Although outraged by his step, the Congress leaders were willing to back Britain with military force *if* Britain gave India independence. The British Conservative government, under Prime Minister Winston Churchill, refused the offer. In 1942 Churchill emphatically stated his case: "I have not become the King's First Minister in order to preside at the liquidation of the British Empire."

In opposition to the Congress leaders, Gandhi disagreed with putting pressure on war-torn Britain. This time, though, Gandhi would offer moral, but no other support to the British. Hitler's genocide of the Jewish people filled him with horror. Didn't nonviolent resistance become utterly powerless when faced with someone like Hitler, he was asked. What happens if your enemy goes on crushing you? Doesn't nonviolence then become senseless sacrifice? To respond with violence, he still said, would only breed more violence. That was not the answer.

Lord Mountbatten, the last viceroy of India, confers with Jawaharlal Nehru in 1948, shortly before India became independent and Nehru its first premier.

Gandhi embraces Muhammad Ali Jinnah, the political leader of India's 100 million Muslims, in September 1944. Jinnah wanted India divided into separate Muslim and Hindu states after independence, and envisaged a future federation of Muslim states embracing parts of China and the Soviet Union.

Indian police, led by British officers, block a nationalist procession outside National Congress headquarters in Bombay during the early 1930s.

The conflict suddenly closed in when the Japanese launched the war in the Pacific. With the attack on Pearl Harbour, the United States entered the war as well. India itself was threatened with invasion as Japanese troops edged towards its borders. Gandhi decided in 1942 that only a free India could defend itself—even nonviolently. The time for compromise was over. He too resorted to pressure tactics. He wanted President Franklin Roosevelt to withhold support from Britain until independence was granted. How can we be asked to fight for freedom if we don't have it, he demanded. "Quit India!" became his slogan.

Gandhi was preparing the country for mass civil disobedience when he and other Congress leaders were imprisoned once again. Kasturbai announced that she would address a meeting in his place in order to get herself arrested, too. As if the trigger

Troops of the Indian army march by the Suez Canal in Egypt in August 1939. During the early days of World War II Britain's Prime Minister Winston Churchill had doubts about the fighting qualities of the Indian army, but his fears proved unfounded when the Indians fought with distinction in North Africa and Italy.

had been pulled, and with no one to control the violence, India went beserk. Indians attacked Britons. The British military attacked Indians.

Famine ensued, killing one and a half million people, even though the British government had made assurances that there would be adequate food supplies. Gandhi fasted in protest for 21 days. Even as he neared death, and the world cried out for his release, the British government refused to budge.

In February 1944, after a long bout with illness, Kasturbai died in Gandhi's lap. As unconventional as it may have been, their marriage and loyalty to each other had lasted 62 years. Six weeks later, Gandhi himself fell seriously ill with malaria. Again,

Prime Minister Churchill confers with two of his senior officers, Lieut.-Col. Sir Sikander Khan and General Sir Archibald Wavell in Cairo, Egypt, in 1942. Wavell, who became viceroy of India in 1943, proved unequal to the demands of Indian politics and was replaced by Lord Mountbatten in 1947.

America's President Roosevelt and Britain's Prime Minister Churchill with Lord Athlone, governor general of Canada, in Quebec, August 18, 1943. In 1942 Gandhi had begged Roosevelt to withold support from Britain until India gained its independence despite the fact that many Indians had fought and died for the British cause during World War II.

A "Quit India" demonstration braves police smoke bombs in Bombay three hours after Gandhi's arrest on August 9, 1942. Demonstrations across India soon turned violent in this campaign, which Gandhi had initiated without consulting either the Muslims or the princely states.

demands for his release pressed in from around the world. When the new viceroy agreed on medical grounds to let him go, Gandhi left prison for the last time. In total, he had spent 2,338 days of his life in prison.

Now Britain had recognized that India's independence was inevitable, the goal of self-rule was threatened from within—by the Muslim League, led by Muhammad Ali Jinnah. An upper-class, English-educated Muslim, Jinnah feared for the rights of the Muslim minority in independent India, but was especially concerned for the economic interests of the Muslim upper-class. Men like Jinnah stood to lose the wealth and prestige they enjoyed under the British. Jinnah was no longer

An Indian soldier kisses the ground upon returning home from fighting in Italy, September 25, 1945.

> *I believe it is possible to introduce uncompromising truth and honesty in the political life of the country... I would strain every nerve to make Truth and Nonviolence accepted in all our national activities.*
>
> —GANDHI

simply demanding special rights, however, but a separate Muslim state to be carved out of India.

To start, there were serious practical problems. Jinnah wanted to form his Muslim state by partitioning off the northwest and northeast parts of India where the Muslim population was concen-

Muhammad Ali Jinnah speaks at a Muslim League meeting in Delhi, April 7, 1946. Determined to achieve an independence settlement favourable to India's Muslims, he said: "We are prepared to sacrifice anything and everything. We shall not submit to any scheme of government prepared without our consent."

Lord and Lady Mountbatten talk with Gandhi in New Delhi on March 31, 1947. Mountbatten, who had arrived in New Delhi on March 22, had summoned Gandhi immediately. Gandhi, however, refused to go to the meeting by plane, considering it improper that he should travel in a way most Indians could never hope to afford.

The parade in New Delhi on
Independence Day, August
15, 1947. A little-pub-
licized aspect of Indian nationalism is in evidence
here—the troops at the
head of the parade are
former members of the In-
dian National Army, who
fought alongside the Japanese armies against the Allies during World War II.

trated, even though a thousand miles of India lay between the two areas. Would all the Muslims in India be forced to give up their homes? Would all the Hindus and other religious groups in the Muslim territories have to leave? The name of the proposed state was Pakistan, which means "land of the pure". In reality Pakistan would spell disaster.

My countrymen impute the evils of modern civilization to the English people and, therefore, believe that the English people are bad, and not the civilization they represent. My countrymen, therefore, believe that they should adopt modern civilization and modern methods of violence to drive out the British.
—GANDHI

Lord Mountbatten takes the salute at a parade marking India's independence in August 1947.

Muslim refugees flee India in September 1947. The terms of India's independence established the new Muslim state of Pakistan in India's former northeastern regions. Religious violence on a massive scale broke out almost immediately, a catastrophe which even Mahatma Gandhi's appeals could not prevent.

Refusing to negotiate with Gandhi, Jinnah put his energy into fuelling Hindu and Muslim hatred and inciting violence. Hindus and Muslims murdered each other by the hundreds in the streets. Appalled, Gandhi turned once again to the people and set out on a barefoot pilgrimage from village to village through the Muslim region of Bengal. At first stones and broken glass were hurled at him, but gradually his presence brought a measure of calm in the strife-torn area.

In 1947 Lord Mountbatten, the last British viceroy, arrived. His goal—to complete the British withdrawal from India. It began to look, however, as though India would collapse into chaos should the British leave. Gandhi told Mountbatten that there would be civil war if India were divided. Jinnah threatened civil war if India were not divided.

Muslim refugees leave New Delhi for the safety of Pakistan in September 1947, making their way past victims of the savage fighting between Muslims and Hindus which followed the partition of India.

Muslims fleeing persecution by Hindus in India cross a bridge near the Pakistan border in September 1947. Gandhi fasted in vain from January 13 to January 18, 1948, for national reconciliation, and even proposed organizing a march from India to Pakistan in an attempt to reunite the country.

Nehru, who had been asked to form a provisional government, agreed to Jinnah's partition plan, hoping to satisfy the Muslims and bring an end to the disorder. He was growing impatient and afraid to delay independence any longer.

On August 15, 1947, India celebrated Independence day. What should have been Gandhi's celebration was not. He refused to attend the ceremonies and spent the day in prayer, alone, at odds with India's leaders, wondering if all his work was to end in failure, and fearing what was still to come.

The Great Migration began. Refugees swarmed in droves from Pakistan into India and from India into

The bed upon which Gandhi fasted in January 1948. Shortly after the end of the fast (which had seriously weakened him), he appealed for religious tolerance in a radio broadcast which was transmitted throughout India and the new state of Pakistan.

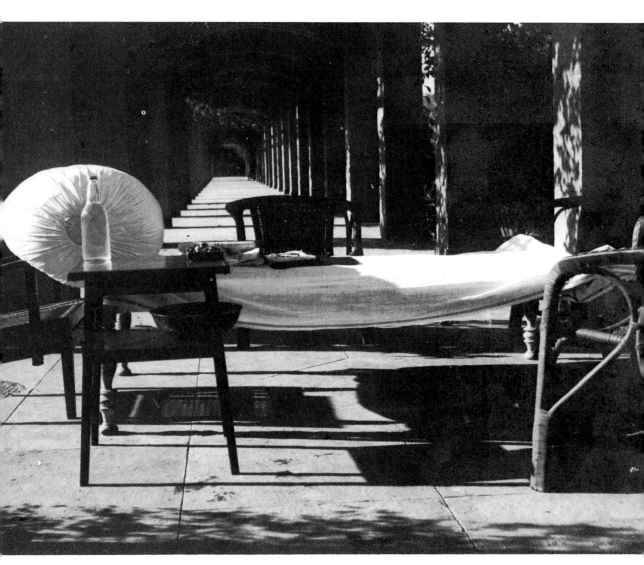

Gandhi, greatly weakened
by fasting, greets his disciples in New Delhi on January 21, 1948.

Pakistan. Mass rioting and fighting rocked both countries. Fifteen million people were left homeless and over half a million dead. Trainloads were massacred at once.

By fasting Gandhi once more gradually managed to calm the rioting and bring a shaky peace. At the same time he was met with rising antagonism. Hindu extremists, angered by his policy of religious tolerance and his tendency as a Hindu to demand more from the Hindus than the Muslims, were turning against him. From Calcutta, where he had fasted, Gandhi continued on his way to the Punjab, where conditions were reported to be horrific, but conditions in Delhi were so terrible that he was forced to stop. Riots raged out of control. Mosques and Muslim neighbourhoods were reduced to burnt rubble. Refugees and dead bodies, victims of

If we want to give the people a sense of freedom we shall have to provide them with work which they can easily do in their desolate homes and which would give them at least the barest living. And when they have become self-reliant and are able to support themselves we are in a position to talk to them about freedom.
—GANDHI

Nathuram Godse, Gandhi's assassin. Godse, a Hindu extremist, was executed for his crime in 1949.

disease as well as bloody violence, filled the streets.

Unable to house himself in the untouchables' slums as usual, Gandhi stayed at the mansion of a wealthy businessman. There he spoke to Nehru, held daily prayer meetings in the garden, and visited refugee camps. His despair was increasing. Once more he fasted for the sake of unity and peace. After six days, religious leaders had signed a pledge but Gandhi hesitated. Signatures were not enough. Could they really convince the people to keep peace? They pleaded tearfully with him. At last Gandhi agreed to stop.

On January 20, 1948, a bomb exploded at Gandhi's prayer meeting. Responsibility was laid on the RRS, a group of terrorist Hindu extremists who wanted to exterminate all Muslims. Gandhi was aware that his life was threatened. He even spoke about the possibility and how he would face it. "If I fall victim to an assassin's bullet", he said, "there must be no anger within me. God must be in my heart and on my lips."

On January 30, still weak from his fast, Gandhi hurried to his prayer meeting, worried because he was a few minutes late. Five hundred people were gathered in the garden. Gandhi bowed low to bless them. A man in front of him bowed in return. His name was Nathuram Godse. A member of the RRS, Godse then lifted a gun and fired three times into Gandhi's stomach and heart. Gandhi fell to the ground. "Hai Rama", he murmured. "Oh God."

"The light has gone out", Nehru told the country over the radio, breaking the news of Gandhi's death. "Perhaps I am wrong to say that. Nevertheless, we will not see him again as we have seen him these many years."

According to Hindu custom, Gandhi's body was cremated and his ashes immersed in India's rivers. His country gave their prophet of peaceful tolerance the highest honour at his funeral—a full military procession. More than a million people of all religions crowded the funeral route, crying "Long live Mahatma Gandhi", united briefly, ironically, in sorrow, by the violent death of a man who had preached nonviolence.

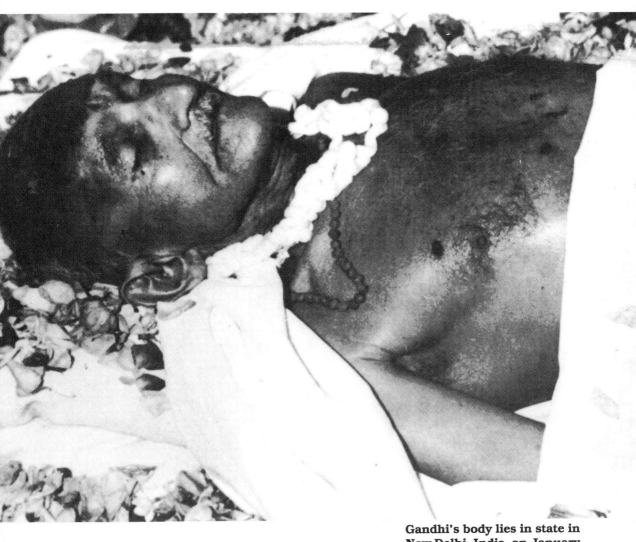

Gandhi's body lies in state in New Delhi, India, on January 30, 1948. Gandhi's funeral was organized by the defence ministry and supervised by Major-General Roy Bucher, British commander-in-chief. It is ironic that even after his death Gandhi could not escape the ministrations of the British.

Gandhi's body, covered with rose petals, is carried through crowds of mourners to the cremation site on January 31, 1948. His son, Ramdas, lit the pyre.

Indian police, soldiers, and volunteer guards beat back the crowds surrounding Gandhi's funeral pyre on January 31, 1948. When the flames rose to their greatest height, the crowd shouted, "The Mahatma has become immortal."

11
After Gandhi

At independence, India became a federal republic within the British Commonwealth. Jawaharlal Nehru continued as prime minister until his death in 1964. He worked to make India a modern nation, to give it status in international affairs and, in opposition to Gandhi's vision, to industrialize the country. Large-scale redistribution of land from land-owners to the peasants also took place, and the caste system was legally abolished, although it has not been wiped out.

Nehru's daughter, Indira Gandhi, who became prime minister in 1966, remained in power until her assassination in 1984. While it was only coincidence that she had married a man with Gandhi's name, it was certainly to her advantage politically. Indira Gandhi's policies bore little resemblance to her namesake's. In 1975, when her power was threatened, she declared a state of national emergency in order to crush her opponents.

In the early 1970s Pakistan split into two countries, Pakistan in the west and Bangladesh in the east, after bitter fighting that left millions dead and sent new tides of refugees into India.

Today India keeps up ties with both the United States and the Soviet Union. It has its own nuclear power plant. The first Indian astronaut took part in

Martin Luther King, the American civil rights leader and advocate of non-violence (who became known in India as the American Gandhi) visits Gandhi's shrine in New Delhi, February 11, 1959.

Crowds gather on the shore at the confluence of the Jumna and Ganges rivers near Allahabad, India, on February 12, 1948, following the immersion of Gandhi's ashes there. According to Hindu belief, an invisible and celestial river shares the same confluence.

The last British troops to leave India parade in Bombay before their departure on February 28, 1948.

a 1984 Soviet mission. Still India remains a country troubled by extreme poverty, overpopulation, food shortages, and a weak economy. Bloody religious conflicts continue to erupt.

Although Gandhi did not completely realize his ideal visions, and insisted there was "no such thing as 'Gandhism'", his impact has been felt all over the globe. The struggles of other Asian and African nations to gain independence from colonial powers have been influenced by his work. In the United States, Dr Martin Luther King, the black civil rights leader, paid tribute to Gandhi's example and created his own American *Satyagraha* to protest against legalized racial discrimination. Like Gandhi, King could not in the end avoid outbreakes of violence and rioting, and like Gandhi, was assassinated.

Gandhi's followers arranged his few possessions in his room at Birla House in Bombay shortly after he died. Seen here are his bedding, his spinning wheel and his writing desk.

The Indian government issued this stamp honouring Martin Luther King in 1969. King, like Gandhi a believer in nonviolence, was assassinated in 1968.

भारत
INDIA

DR. MARTIN LUTHER KING

डा. मार्टिन लूथर किंग 1929-1968

पै.
P. 20

Through Dr King's struggle for black rights, Gandhi came to the attention of one generation of Americans. Now, through an Academy Award-winning film by Richard Attenborough, Gandhi's life and work has captured the imagination of a new generation. Gandhi is not about to be forgotten, it seems. In the age we live in, with the human race having the capacity to destroy life on this planet, Gandhi's example of trust, tolerance, and protest by nonviolent means may be crucial to our survival. As long as there is hope for humanity, Gandhi's light will not go out.

Mahatma Gandhi was the spokesman for the conscience of all mankind.
—GENERAL GEORGE C. MARSHALL,
U.S. Secretary of State

Gandhi in 1946, photographed by the renowned
American photographer Margaret Bourke-White.

Further Reading

Ashe, Geoffrey. *Gandhi: A Study in Revolution.* London: Heinemann, 1968.

Catlin, George. *In the Path of Mahatma Gandhi.* London: Macdonald & Co., 1948.

Cheney, Glenn Alan. *Mohandas Gandhi.* New York: Franklin Watts, 1983.

Fischer, Louis. *The Life of Mohandas Gandhi.* New York: Harper & Row, 1950.

Gandhi, Mohandas K. *Moral and Political Writings*, vols 1–3. Oxford: Oxford University Press, 1987.

Mehta, Ved. *Mahatma Gandhi and his Apostles.* London: Andre Deutsch, 1977.

Woodcock, George. *Gandhi.* London: Fontana, 1972.

A picture of Gandhi adorns the floor of the Bombay building which served as his headquarters between 1919 and 1934. The figure of Buddha and the Christian cross demonstrate Gandhi's followers' conviction that he was the spiritual successor of both Christ and the Buddha.

Chronology

Oct. 2, 1869	Gandhi is born in Porbandar
1885	Indian National Congress founded
1888	Gandhi travels to London to study law
April 1893	Gandhi arrives in South Africa
May 1894	Gandhi founds the Natal Indian Congress
1899	Boer War in South Africa
	Gandhi founds an ambulance corps to support the British
July 1907	The Transvaal Asiatic Registration Act becomes law
	Gandhi launches a *Satyagraha* campaign
Aug. 16, 1908	Gandhi addresses mass meeting in Johannesburg and encourages burning of registration certificates
1914	Gandhi and Smuts negotiate the Indian Relief Act
Jan. 9, 1915	Gandhi returns to India
April 6, 1919	Gandhi initiates nationwide *hartal*
April 13, 1919	Amritsar massacre
1920	Gandhi reorganizes Congress Party and begins *Satyagraha* campaign
1922	Gandhi is imprisoned for two years
1924	Gandhi conducts a fast for Hindu Muslim unity
1930	The Salt March and *Satyagraha* campaign
March 4, 1931	Irwin and Gandhi sign the Delhi Pact
Sept. 1931	Round Table Conference in London
1942	"Quit India" campaign
March 22, 1947	Lord Mountbatten, the last viceroy, arrives in India
Aug. 15, 1947	India becomes independent
	Nehru becomes prime minister
Jan. 30, 1948	Gandhi is assassinated by Nathuram Godse
1966	Indira Gandhi becomes prime minister
Oct. 31, 1984	Indira Gandhi assassinated by a Sikh extremist
Dec. 29, 1984	Indira Gandhi's son Rajiv is elected prime minister

Index